# BRAIN GAME

MW00954828

# Get Ready to
# READ

## Picture Puzzles
## for Growing Minds

My shoe is red.

Publications International, Ltd.

Images from Shutterstock.com

Brain Games is a registered trademark of Publications International, Ltd.

Louis Weber, CEO
Publications International, Ltd.
8140 Lehigh Avenue
Morton Grove, IL 60053

Permission is never granted for commercial purposes.

ISBN: 978-1-64558-843-6

Manufactured in China.

8 7 6 5 4 3 2 1

# What is STEM?

The acronym STEM stands for Science, Technology, Engineering, and Math. STEM is not just about knowledge, but about how to obtain, process, and apply that knowledge. Introducing these concepts early on can help foster children's curiosity and build the skills they need to understand the world around them.

# Play to LEARN.

The picture puzzles in this book encourage children to explore and learn, even as they play! Puzzlers improve their print awareness, knowledge of letters and sounds, sight-word vocabulary, and other literacy skills by using observation, critical thinking, and problem-solving. Throughout the book, bright, colorful pictures and challenging games keep children interested and entertained.

The puzzles may be done in any order, and with or without help from an adult. Kids can use the table of contents to find their favorite types of puzzles or dive straight in!

# Contents

# Contents

# At the Start

Which of these starts with the letter S?

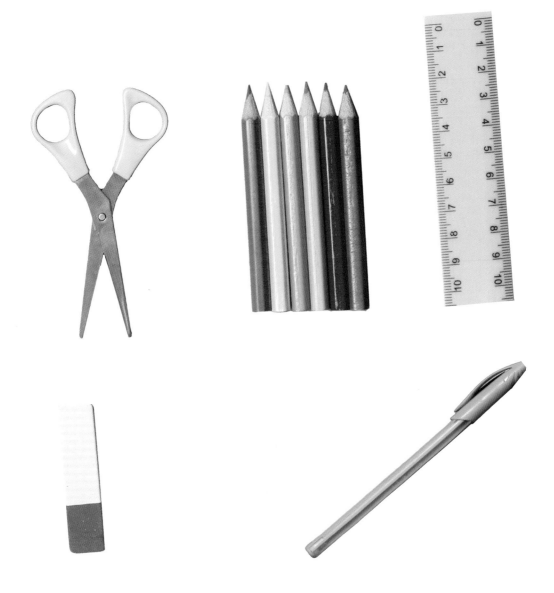

*Answers on page 105.*

# Shapes and Colors

Fill in each shape with the right color.

Color the star red.
Color the circle blue.
Color the X pink.

  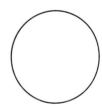

 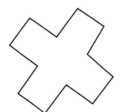 

# Filling In

What letter is missing from the word?

C_T

*Answers on page 105.*

# Do It!

Tilt this book! What will happen to the teapot?
Turn the page to find out.

What happened? Were you right?

*Answers on page 105.*

# Hide and Seek

Find the crayon hiding in the blocks.

# Secret Code

The word below is in code. Each symbol stands for a letter. Using the key, write each letter above the matching symbol.

△ □ ⬡ ☆ ♥

△ =F ■ =R

♥ =T ☆ =I ⬡ =U

*Answers on page 106.*

# Hidden Pattern

Look for this pattern of pictures inside the big grid.

# Clues

I spot an animal! Use the clues to figure out which animal I see.

I have fur.

I have a fluffy tail

I have big feet and big ears.

*Answers on page 106.*

# On the Right Path

Follow the path that goes through every uppercase letter. But avoid the lowercase letters!

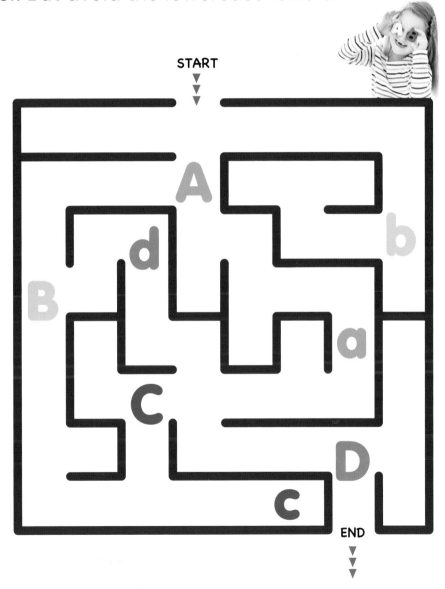

# Knowing Names

What color is the slime? Circle the right color.

Yellow **Purple** Green

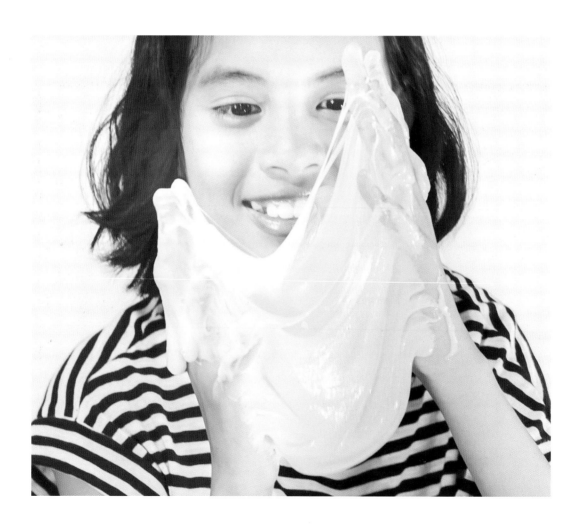

*Answers on page 107.*

# Color by Letter

What does this picture show? Fill each letter's space with the matching color to find out.

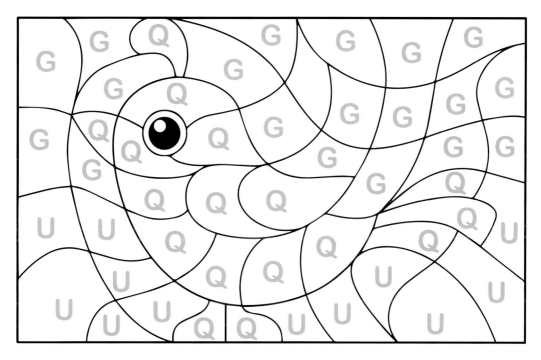

Was your guess right?

# Filling In

What letter is missing from the word?

__EBRA

*Answers on page 107.*

# What Am I?

What do you think this picture is? Connect the dots to find out.

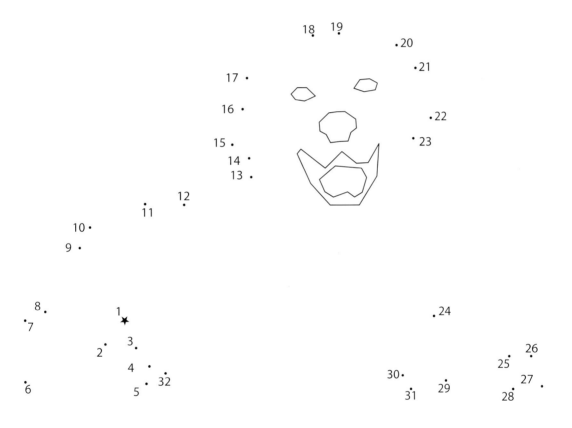

## Was your guess right?

*Answers on page 108.*

# Letter Hunt

Words are everywhere!

Look around you at school, at home, and anywhere else. Can you find each letter that is listed on these pages?

What words did you find the letters in? Write down the words.

L _____

M_____

O _____

P _____

K _____

S _____

A _____

F _____

*Answers on page 108.*

# At the Start

Which of these starts with the letter L?

*Answers on page 108.*

# Find Me

Circle the 2 B blocks in the picture.

# Secret Code

A word below is in code. Each symbol stands for a letter. Using the key, write each letter above the matching symbol.

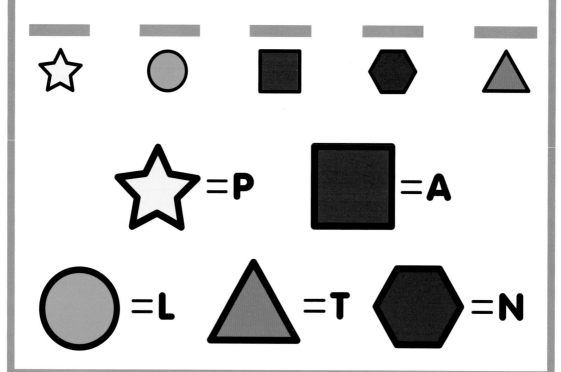

☆ =P  ■ =A

● =L  ▲ =T  ⬡ =N

*Answers on page 109.*

# Match It

Draw a line from each uppercase letter to its lowercase letter.

A                    c

B                    d

C                    a

D                    b

# Follow the Code

Follow each step to make the smoothie.

*Answers on page 109.*

# What Am I?

What do you think this picture is? Connect the dots to find out.

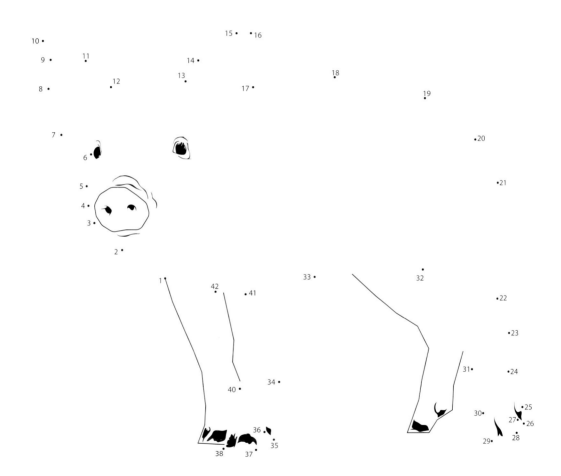

Was your guess right?

# Knowing Names

What kind of animals are these? Circle the right name.

## Dogs   Birds   Horses

*Answers on page 110.*

# Which Ones?

Circle all 3 numbers you can find in this picture.

# Clues

I can't find my vehicle. Use the clues to figure out which one is mine.

It has 4 wheels.

It is yellow.

It has a big scoop in front.

*Answers on page 110.*

# At the Start

Which of these starts with the letter H?

# Shapes and Colors

Fill in each shape with the right color.

Color the a diamond yellow.
Color the star purple.
Color the oval orange.

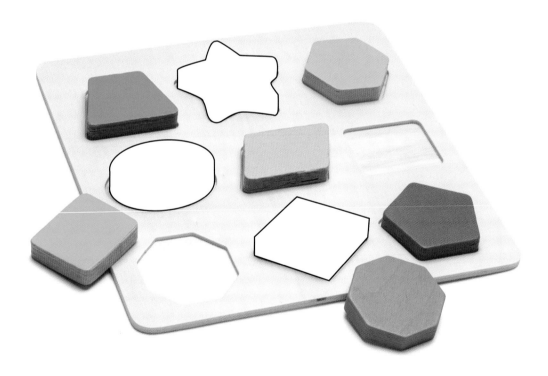

*Answers on page 111.*

# Filling In

What letter is missing from the word?

## _OOKS

# Hide and Seek

Find the items hiding in the school supplies.

*Answers on page 111.*

# Secret Code

A word below is in code. Each symbol stands for a letter. Using the key, write each letter above the matching symbol.

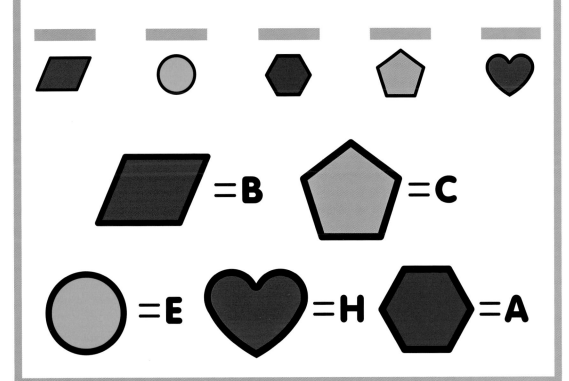

= B    = C

= E    = H    = A

# Hidden Pattern

Look for this pattern of pictures inside the big grid.

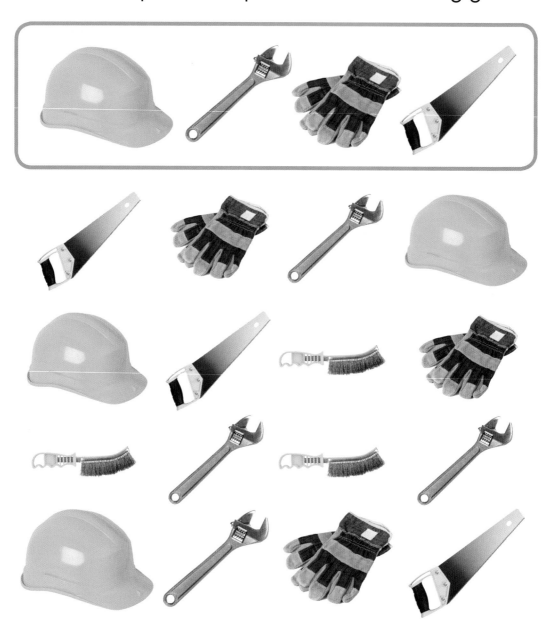

Answers on page 112.

# Clues

I lost my favorite block. Use the clues to figure out which one is my favorite.

> It is red.
>
> It has four sides.

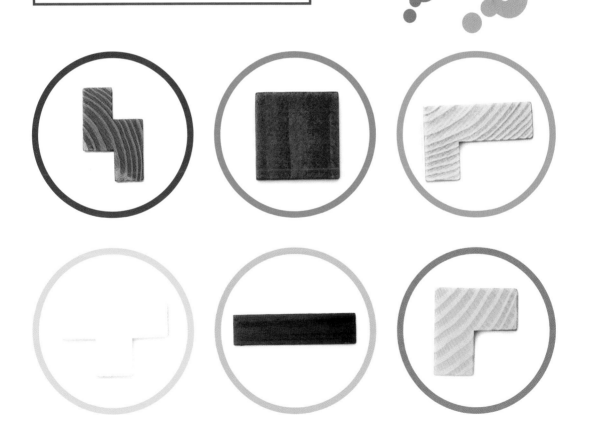

# On the Right Path

Follow the path that goes through every red flower. But avoid the numbers!

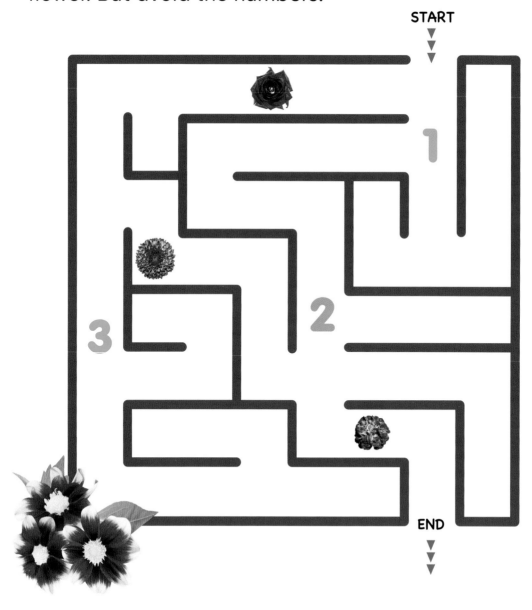

START

1

3

2

END

*Answers on page 112.*

# Knowing Names

What color is the shoe? Circle the correct color.

## Red   Blue   Purple

# Color by Letter

What does this picture show? Fill each letter's space with the matching color to find out.

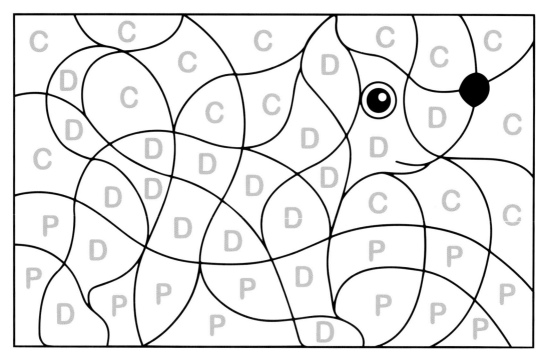

Was your guess right?

*Answers on page 113.*

# Filling In

What letter is missing from the word?

# What Am I?

What do you think this picture is? Connect the dots to find out.

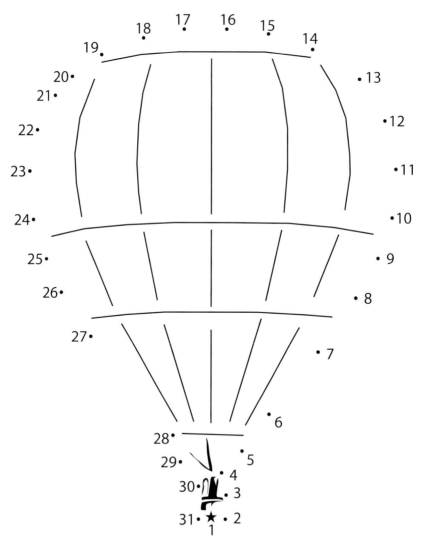

Were you right?

*Answers on page 113.*

# At the Start

Which of these starts with the letter S?

*Answers on page 113.*

# Find Me

Circle the 4 ladybugs in the picture.

*Answers on page 114.*

# Secret Code

A word below is in code. Each symbol stands for a letter. Using the key, write each letter above the matching symbol.

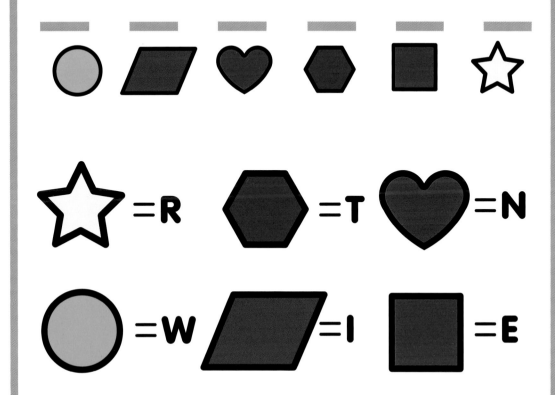

☆ =R    ⬡ =T    ♥ =N

⬤ =W    ▱ =I    ◼ =E

# Match It

Draw a line from each word to its number.

ONE

TWO

THREE

FOUR

2

3

4

1

46

*Answers on page 114.*

# Follow the Code

Follow each step to walk the dog.

| | |
|---|---|
| **1** | START 🥣 |
| **2** | GO ◀ 4 spots to 🦴 |
| **3** | GO ▼ 2 spots to 🪢 |
| **4** | GO ▶ 4 spots to 💩 |

# What Am I?

What do you think this picture is? Connect the dots to find out.

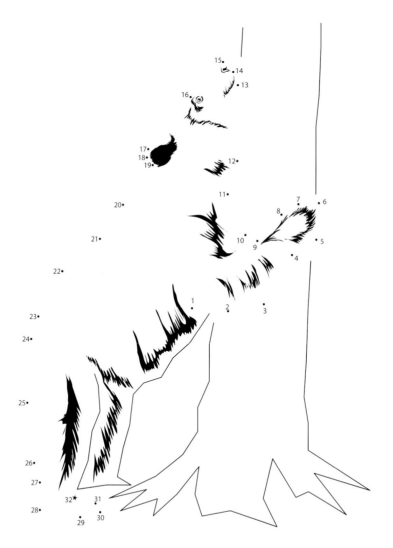

Was your guess right?

Answers on page 115.

# Knowing Names

What is the chipmunk doing? Circle the correct answer.

**Eating**   **Jumping**   **Sleeping**

# Which Ones?

Circle all 4 triangles you can find in this picture.

*Answers on page 115.*

# Clues

I need a tool to finish my yardwork. Use the clues to figure out which tool I need.

> It has a big handle.
>
> It has wheels.
>
> It is red.

# At the Start

Which of these starts with the letter L?

*Answers on page 116.*

# Shapes and Colors

Fill in each shape with the right color.

- Color the D orange.
- Color the M blue.
- Color the O green.
- Color the Z red.

# Filling In

What letters are missing from the word?

## SH_ _P

*Answers on page 116.*

# Do It!

Blow on this book! What will happen to the umbrella? Turn the page to find out.

What happened? Were you right?

*Answers on page 116.*

# Hide and Seek

Circle the wooden spoon in the picture.

# Secret Code

A word below is in code. Each symbol stands for a letter. Using the key, write each letter above the matching symbol.

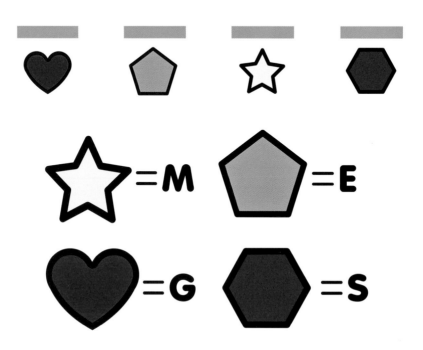

☆ = M    ⬠ = E

♥ = G    ⬡ = S

*Answers on page 117.*

# Hidden Pattern

Look for this pattern of pictures inside the big grid.

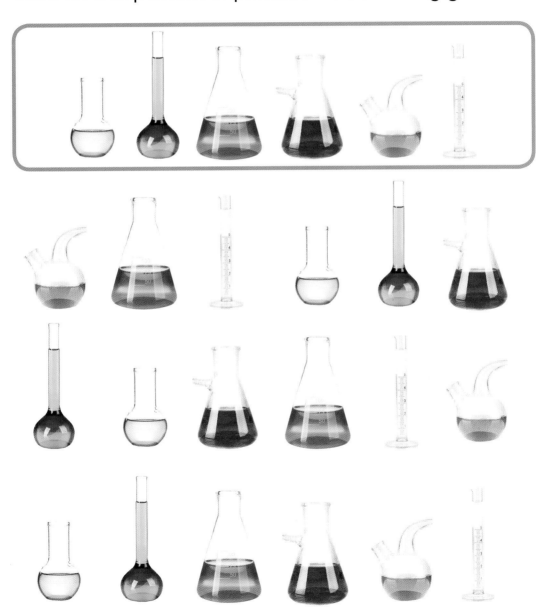

# Clues

An insect just landed by my window. Use the clues to figure out which insect it is.

It has 6 legs.

It has black eyes.

It is green.

*Answers on page 117.*

# On the Right Path

Follow the path that goes through each number. But avoid the letters!

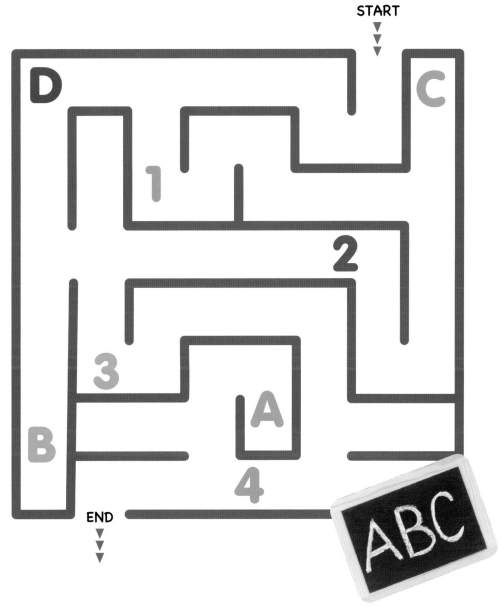

# Knowing Names

What is the girl in the middle looking through? Circle the correct answer.

## Microscope Pencil Marker

*Answers on page 118.*

# Color by Letter

What does this picture show? Fill each letter's space with the matching color to find out.

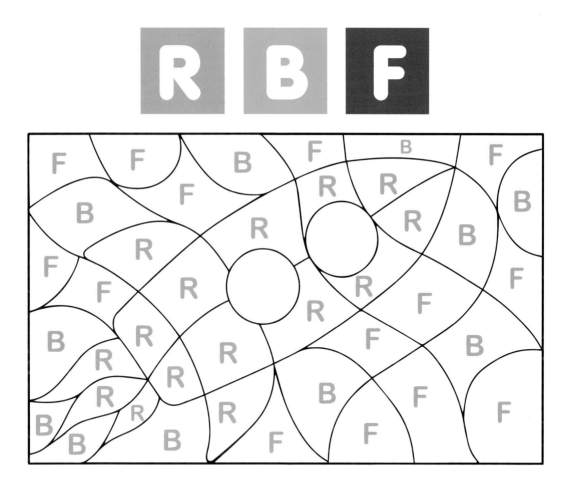

Was your guess right?

# Filling In

What letter is missing from the word?

_REE

*Answers on page 118.*

# What Am I?

What do you think this picture is? Connect the dots to find out.

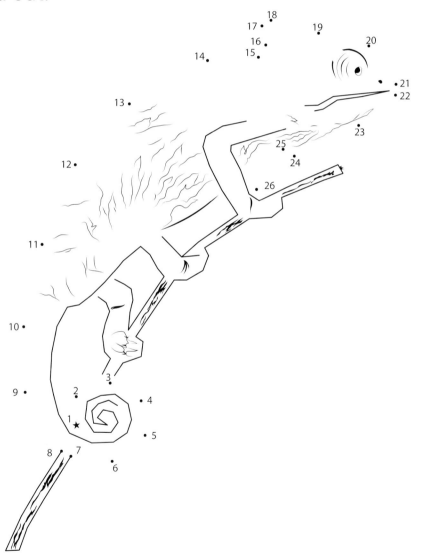

Was your guess right?

# Mix and Match

How many sentences can you make with just a few words?

## What you need:

- 16 index cards
- Black marker or crayon
- Blue marker or crayon
- Red marker or crayon
- Green marker or crayon

## Directions:

**1.** Write each of these phrases in **black** on a different index card:

**The cow**                              **A cat**

**Humpty Dumpty**                        **My hat**

**2.** Write each of these words in blue on a different index card:

jumps                                    sleeps

sits                                     is

**3.** Write each of these in **red** on a different index card:

over                                     in

on                                       under

**4.** Write each of these phrases in **green** on a different index card:

the moon                                 this box

a wall                                   that desk

**5.** Mix all the cards up together, then pick 1 card of each color.

**6.** Read each of your 4 words aloud.

**7.** Put your cards in order so they make a sentence. (If you need a hint, look at the bottom of this page.) Write your sentence:

_____  _____  _____  _____

**8.** Put your cards back into the pile and mix the cards up.

**9.** Choose 4 new cards, 1 of each color. Make a new sentence.

_____  _____  _____  _____

**10.** Try the activity 2 more times with 2 new sets of cards. (You can do more if you want!) Write the sentences you make.

_____  _____  _____  _____

_____  _____  _____  _____

**Extra challenge!**
Can you draw a picture to go with each sentence?

Hint! Try this order: black, blue, red, green.

# At the Start

Which of these starts with the letter D?

*Answers on page 119.*

# Find Me

Find the 3 items hiding in this picture.

# Secret Code

A word below is in code. Each symbol stands for a letter. Using the key, write each letter above the matching symbol.

___ ___ ___ ___ ___

△ =L    ■ =B

☆ =C    ● =O    ⬠ =K

*Answers on page 120.*

# Match It

Draw a line from each word to its picture.

**ROBOT**

**PEPPER**

**ROCK**

**LIGHT**

# Follow the Code

Follow each step to make the burger.

**1** START

**2** GO ▼ 4 spots to

**3** GO ▶ 3 spots to

**4** GO ▲ 2 spots to

**5** GO ▶ 1 spot to

**6** GO ▲ 2 spots to

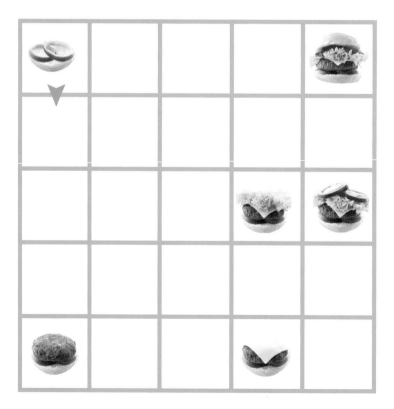

*Answers on page 120.*

# What Am I?

What do you think this picture is? Connect the dots to find out.

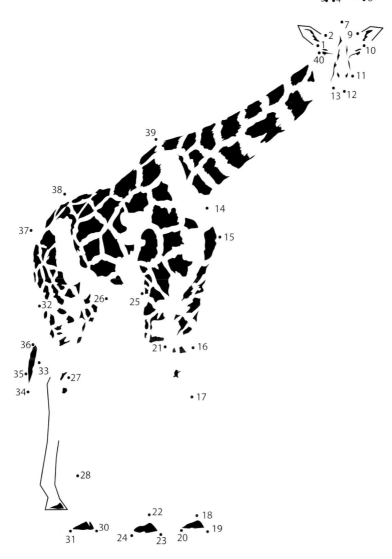

Was your guess right?

Answers on page 120.

# Knowing Names

What animal is this? Circle the correct answer.

## Seal  Dog  **Lion**

*Answers on page 121.*

# Which Ones?

Circle all 8 red fruits and veggies you can find in this picture.

# Clues

I need to go home. Use the clues to figure out which is my home planet.

It has no rings.

It is part blue.

It is part green.

You live on it.

NEPTUNE

MARS          MERCURY          VENUS

JUPITER          EARTH          SATURN

*Answers on page 121.*

# At the Start

Which of these starts with the letter H?

*Answers on page 121.*

# Shapes and Colors

Fill in each shape with the right color.

Color the triangles blue.
Color the arch orange.
Color the rectangle red.

*Answers on page 122.*

# Filling In

What letter is missing from the word?

# Hide and Seek

Circle the glasses in the picture.

*Answers on page 122.*

# Secret Code

A word below is in code. Each symbol stands for a letter. Using the key, write each letter above the matching symbol.

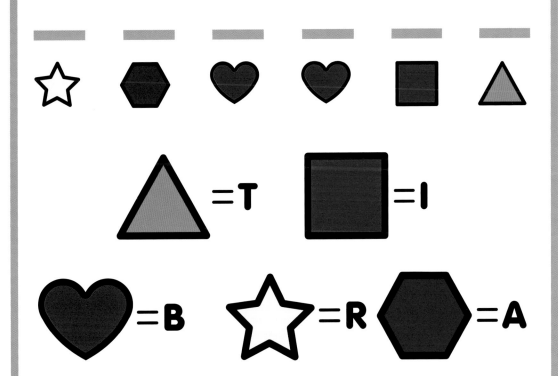

# Hidden Pattern

Look for this pattern of pictures inside the big grid.

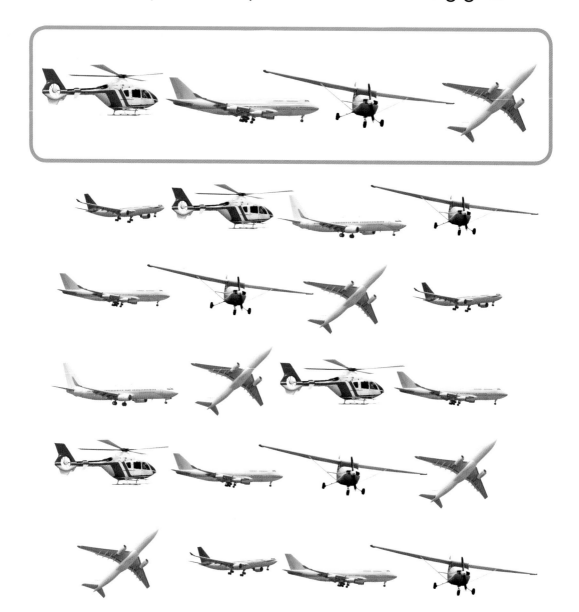

*Answers on page 123.*

# Clues

I have a new job. Use the clues to figure out which person is me.

> I wear a white outfit.
>
> I check if you are healthy.
>
> I work in a hospital.

# On the Right Path

Follow the path that goes through every letter. But avoid the numbers!

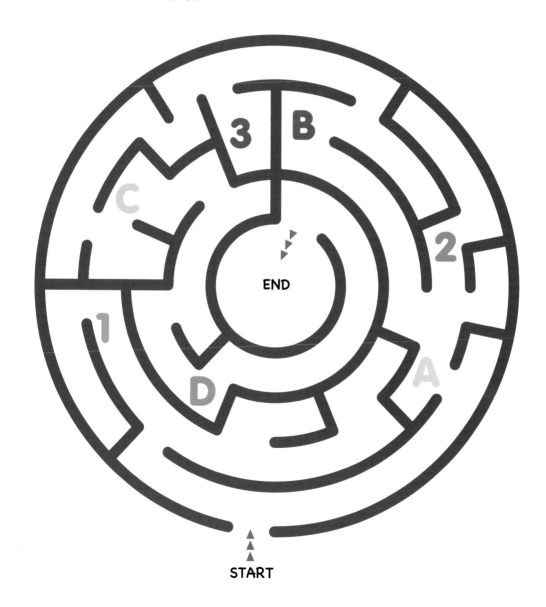

84

Answers on page 123.

# Knowing Names

How many kids are throwing paper airplanes? Circle the correct answer.

Two   Four   Five

# Color by Letter

What does this picture show? Fill each letter's space with the matching color to find out.

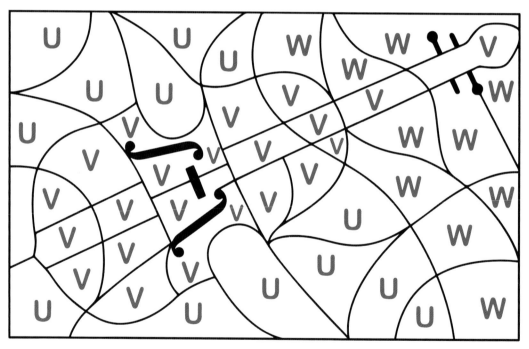

Was your guess right?

Answers on page 124.

# Filling In

What letter is missing from the word?

## \_RUCK

# What Am I?

What do you think this picture is? Connect the dots to find out.

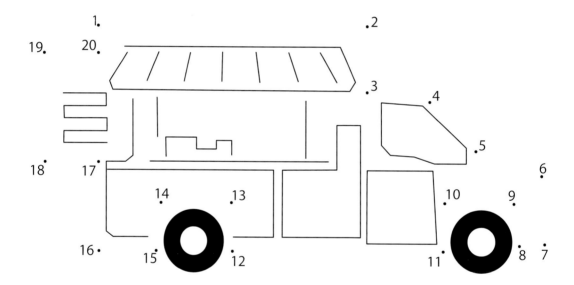

Was your guess right?

Answers on page 124.

# At the Start

Which of these starts with the letter T?

# Find Me

Find the 3 items hiding in the picture.

*Answers on page 125.*

# Secret Code

A word below is in code. Each symbol stands for a letter. Using the key, write each letter above the matching symbol.

$\triangle$ = U  $\blacksquare$ = B  $\blacklozenge$ = S

# Match It

Draw a line from each word to its picture.

**MITTEN**

**DRESS**

**HAT**

**SHIRT**

*Answers on page 125.*

# Follow the Code

Follow each step to get ready for school.

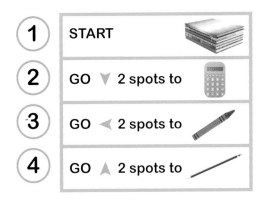

| | |
|---|---|
| 1 | START |
| 2 | GO ▼ 2 spots to |
| 3 | GO ◄ 2 spots to |
| 4 | GO ▲ 2 spots to |

| | |
|---|---|
| 5 | GO ◄ 2 spots to |
| 6 | GO ▼ 4 spots to |

1+1=2    1+6=7
1+2=3    1+7=8
1+3=4    1+8=9
1+4=5    1+9=10
1+5=6    1+10=11

# What Am I?

What do you think this picture is? Connect the dots to find out.

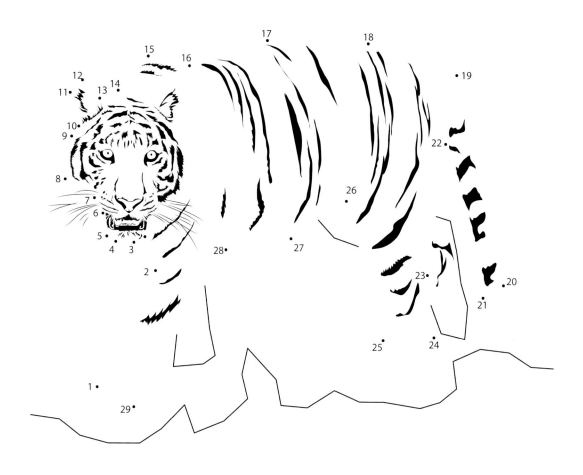

Was your guess right?

Answers on page 126.

# Knowing Names

What animal is this? Circle the correct answer.

## Snake  Monkey  Turtle

# Which Ones?

Circle all 7 green items you can find on this page.

*Answers on page 126.*

# Clues

I need a snack. Use the clues to figure out which food I'm going to eat.

It is green.

It has leaves.

It grows in a big bunch.

# At the Start

Which of these starts with the letter G?

*Answers on page 127.*

# Shapes and Colors

Fill in each shape with the right color.

- Color the star yellow.
- Color the circle blue.
- Color the oval pink.
- Color the rectangle red.
- Color the trapezoid green.

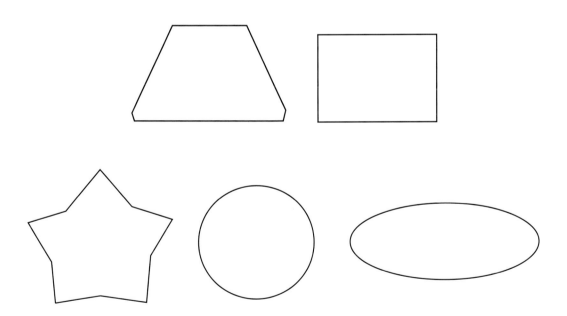

# Filling In

What letter is missing from the word?

FEATHE__

*Answers on page 127.*

# Do It!

Wave this book in the air! What will happen to the kite? Turn the page to find out.

What happened? Were you right?

*Answers on page 127.*

# Hide and Seek

Circle the tiny boat in the picture.

# Secret Code

A word below is in code. Each symbol stands for a letter. Using the key, write each letter above the matching symbol.

❤ = L ⭐ = A ● = B

*Answers on page 128.*

## At the Start: page 6

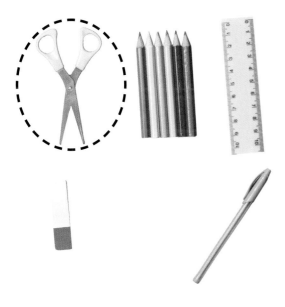

## Filling In: page 8

CAT

## Shapes and Colors: page 7

## Do It!: pages 9-10
The tea was poured into a cup.

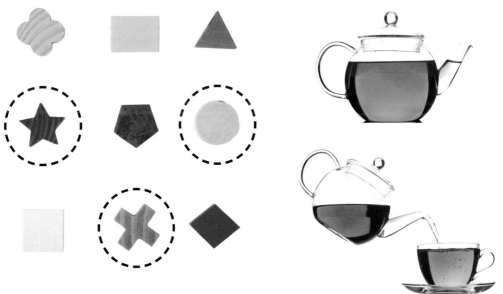

## Hide and Seek: page 11

## Hidden Pattern: page 13

## Secret Code: page 12

**F** **R** **U** **I** **T**

## Clues: page 14

## Zoom In: page 15

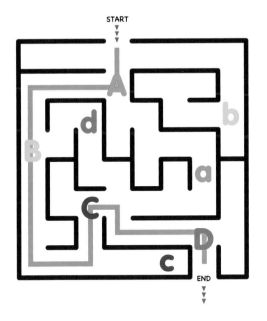

## Color by Letter: page 17

It's a bird.

## Knowing Names: page 16

Yellow  **Purple**  Green

## What Fits?: page 18

## Draw It: page 19

It's a dog.

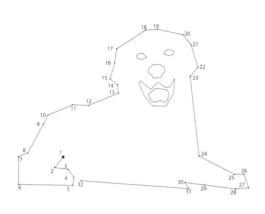

## At the Start: page 22

## Letter Hunt: pages 20–21

Answers vary.

## Hide and Seek: page 23

## Secret Code: page 24

## Follow the Code: page 26

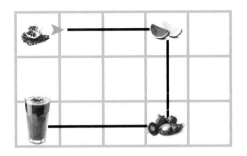

## Match It: page 25

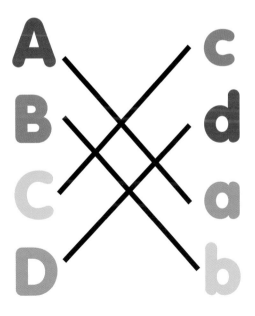

## What Am I?: page 27
It's a pig.

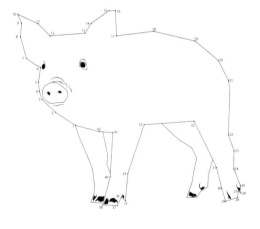

## Knowing Names: page 28

Dogs **Birds** Horses

## Clues: page 30

## Which Ones?: page 29

## At the Start: page 31

## Shapes and Colors: page 32

## Hide and Seek: page 34

## Filling In: page 33

**B**OOKS

## Find It: page 35

B E A C H

## Hidden Patterns: page 36

## On the Right Path: page 38

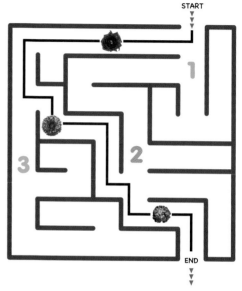

## Clues: page 37

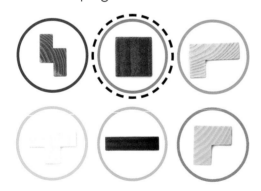

## Knowing Names: page 39

**Red** Blue Purple

## Color by Letter: page 40
It's a dog.

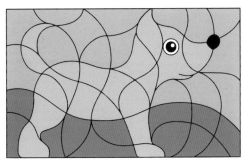

## What Am I?: page 42
It's a hot air balloon.

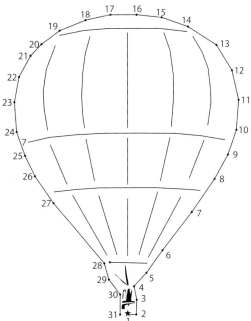

## Filling In: page 41

## At the Start: page 43

## Find Me: page 44

## Match It: page 46

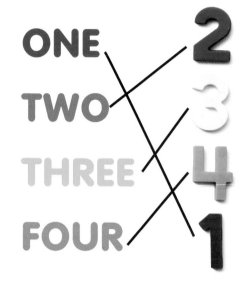

## Secret Code: page 45

## Follow the Code: page 47

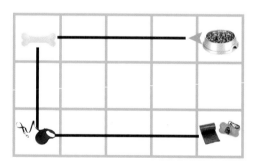

## What Am I: page 48

It's a bear.

## Which Ones?: page 50

## Knowing Names: page 49

**Eating**   **Jumping**   **Sleeping**

## Clues: page 51

# Answers

## At the Start: page 52

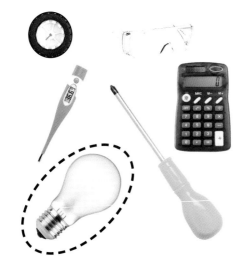

## Filling In: page 54

**SHE E P**

## Shapes and Colors: page 53

## Do It!: pages 55–56
The umbrella was blown inside out.

## Hide and Seek: page 57

## Hidden Pattern: page 59

## Secret Code: page 58

**G E M S**

## Clues: page 60

## On the Right Path:
page 61

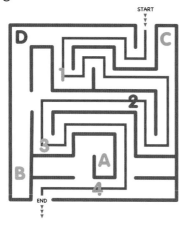

## Color by Shapes: page 63
It's a rocket ship.

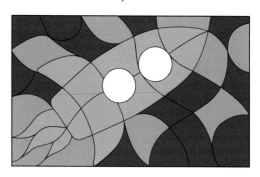

## Knowing Names: page 62

(Microscope) Pencil **Marker**

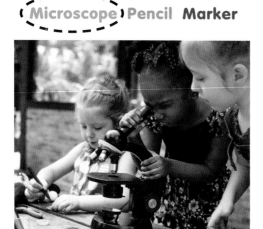

## Filling In: pages 64

**TREE**

## What Am I?: page 65

It's a lizard (a chameleon).

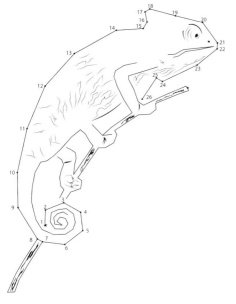

## At the Start: page 68

## Mix and Match: pages 66-67

- Answers vary. Examples:

- The cow jumped over the moon.

- Humpty Dumpty sits on a wall.

- A cat sleeps in this box.

- My hat is under that desk.

## Find Me: page 69

## Secret Code: page 70

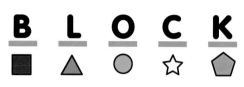

B L O C K

■ ▲ ● ☆ ⬠

## Follow the Code: page 72

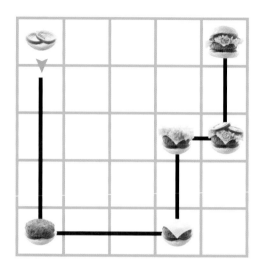

## Match It: page 71

ROBOT

PEPPER

ROCK

LIGHT

## What Am I?: page 73
It's a giraffe.

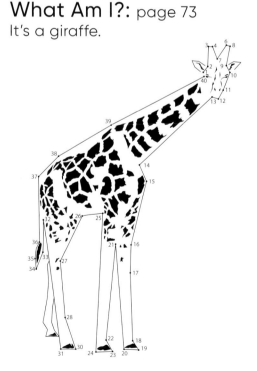

## Knowing Names: page 74

(Seal) Dog **Lion**

## Clues: page 76

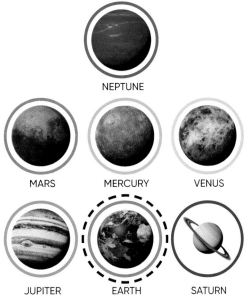

NEPTUNE

MARS     MERCURY     VENUS

JUPITER     EARTH     SATURN

## Which Ones?: page 75

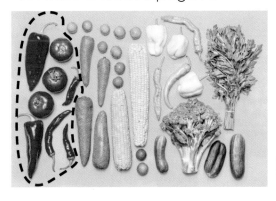

## At the Start: page 77

## Shapes and Colors: page 78

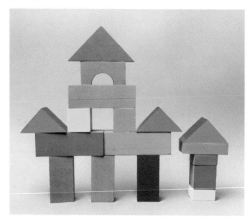

## Hide and Seek: page 80

## Filling In: page 79

**LEAF**

## Secret Code: page 81

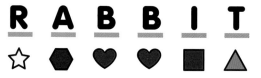

R A B B I T

## Hidden Pattern: page 82

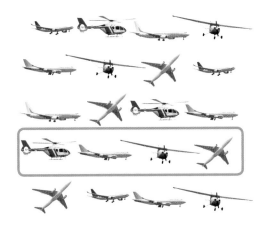

## On the Right Path: page 84

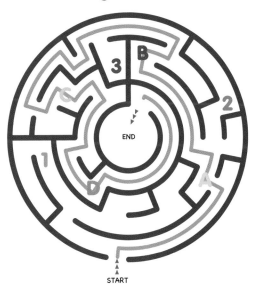

## Clues: page 83

## Knowing Names: page 85

Two  Four  Five

## Color By Letter: page 86
It's a violin.

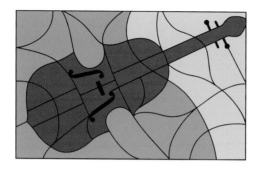

## What Am I?: page 88
It's a truck.

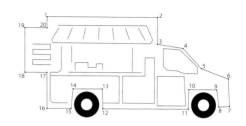

## Filling In: page 87

**TRUCK**

## At the Start: page 89

## Find Me: page 90

## Match It: page 92

MITTEN

DRESS

HAT

SHIRT

## Secret Code: page 91

**B U S**

## Follow the Code: page 93

## What Am I?: page 94
It's a tiger.

## Which Ones?: page 96

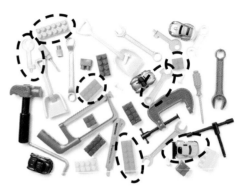

## Knowing Names: page 95

**Snake**  *Monkey*  (Turtle)

## Clues: page 97

## At the Start: page 98

## Filling In: page 100

**FEATHER**

## Shapes and Colors:
page 99

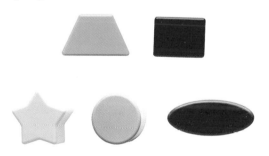

## Do It!: pages 101–102
The kite flew into the air.

Answers

## Hide and Seek: pages 103

## Secret Code: pages 104

**B** **A** **L** **L**